Tudor Theatre

Moira Butterfield

FRANKLIN WATTS

This edition published in 2013 by Franklin Watts

Copyright © Franklin Watts 2013

Franklin Watts
338 Euston Road
London NW1 3BH

Franklin Watts Australia
Level 17/207 Kent Street
Sydney NSW 2000

A CIP catalogue record for this book
is available from the British Library.

Dewey number: 792'.0942

ISBN 978 1 4451 1858 1

Printed in China

Franklin Watts is a division of Hachette Children's Books,
an Hachette UK company.

www.hachette.co.uk

Designer: Jason Billin
Editor: Sarah Ridley
Art director: Jonathan Hair
Editor-in-chief: John C. Miles
Picture research: Diana Morris

Note to parents and teachers:
Every effort has been made by the Publishers to ensure
that the websites in this book are suitable for children, that
they are of the highest educational value, and that they
contain no inappropriate or offensive material. However,
because of the nature of the Internet, it is impossible to
guarantee that the contents of these sites will not be
altered. We strongly advise that Internet access is
supervised by a responsible adult.

Contents

The first theatres

The first British theatre was built in the 16th century during the reign of England's Queen Elizabeth I (1558–1603).

Before theatres

Before theatres were built bands of travelling players (actors) toured the country. They would put on shows in town squares, inns and large houses. They performed Bible stories or popular legends, such as Robin Hood.

Theatre is born

In 1576 the first permanent theatre was built, in Shoreditch, London. It was round-shaped, with balconies for the audience, overlooking the stage.

Queen Elizabeth I loved watching plays and encouraged theatres and playwrights.

Key fact

Elizabeth I belonged to the Tudor family, who reigned for 118 years. James I, from the Stuart family, became king on Elizabeth's death.

People could pay less to stand in the pit — the space in front of the stage — than those seated to watch the show. They were called "groundlings".

Theatre is a hit

Groups of actors called "companies" formed in London and more theatres were built for them. They were only allowed to perform with permission from royal officials, so they had to make sure their work pleased the Queen and her nobles.

Did you know?

The most famous playwright from this time is William Shakespeare (see pages 22–23).

Go and visit

Travelling players often performed outdoors. You can still see performances of Shakespeare's plays outdoors every summer all around the country.

These travelling players are performing on a temporary stage in the courtyard of an inn.

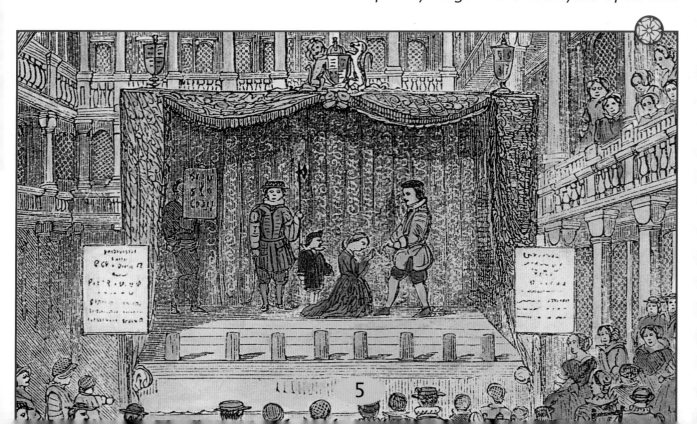

Off to see a play

London was the biggest city in Britain in Tudor times. It became the centre of theatre life.

Theatres mean trouble

The main entertainment area was Bankside, a road along the south bank of the River Thames in an area called Southwark. Several theatres were built there, including Shakespeare's theatre, the Globe (see top panel on page 7). Plays were banned in the City of London, on the north bank of the Thames, because city officials thought they caused riots and bad behaviour.

This drawing shows the original Globe Theatre, on Bankside in London.

Party across the river

Playgoers could walk across London Bridge or pay a penny to catch a ferry across the Thames to see a play. Once in Southwark they could also go to taverns for a drink or see cock-fights (fights between cockerels), or visit a bear-baiting pit to see a chained bear fight a pack of dogs.

6

Did you know?

Richard Burbage once saved a theatre from being destroyed by City of London officials because it was inside their walls. He had the whole building secretly dismantled in the middle of the night and took it over the river to rebuild it. It became the first Globe Theatre.

Come to the play

When a play was going to be performed, a flag flew on top of the theatre for everybody to see. Shows were held in the afternoon, so the audience could get home before dark. There were no plays on Sundays or for two months in summer, when London was a hot, stinking, unhealthy place.

 ## Go and visit

The Museum of London, near London Wall in the City of London. Here you can see real everyday Tudor items on display and examine a model of another Tudor theatre called the Rose.

 ## Key fact

The London theatres had to close whenever there were outbreaks of deadly plague in London. Then the actors went on tour and put on performances in other towns.

This sketch was made in 1590 and shows the stage and some of the seating in a theatre called the Swan, also on Bankside.

Inside a theatre

The most well-known Elizabethan theatre is the Globe, where many of William Shakespeare's plays were first performed.

The Globe has now been carefully reconstructed on a site near its original location. The reconstruction has been based on drawings and diaries that describe original theatres of the time.

*This model of a Tudor theatre shows the stage **1**, the gallery for musicians or wealthy nobles **2** and the seating in covered balconies **3**.*

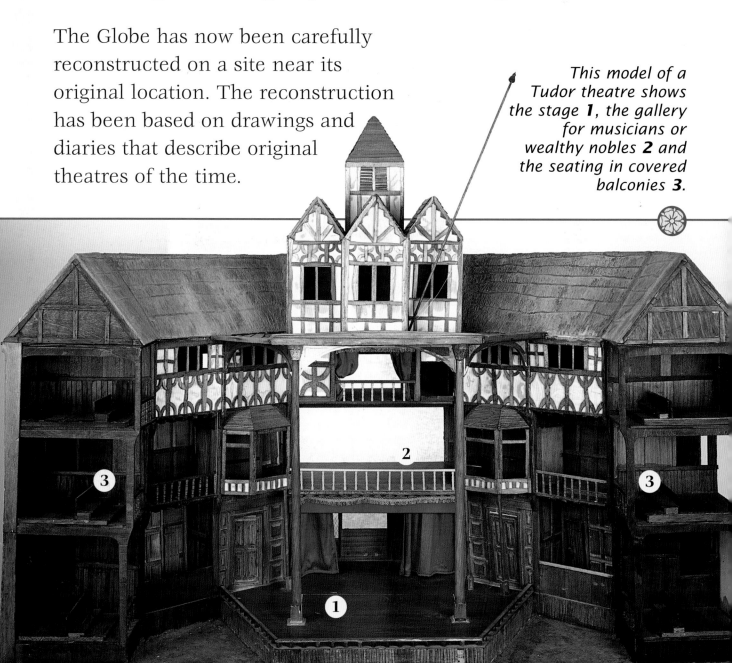

Go and visit

The Globe Theatre in London. It has a museum all about Elizabethan theatre life. You can visit the stage, which looks like an original of the time.

Exciting effects

The first theatres were round and partly open to the sky. The stage jutted out into the middle under a small roof that was painted with stars and clouds to look like the heavens. It had ropes to "fly" actors or props down from above, and a trapdoor in the stage for actors to appear and disappear. Fireworks and smoke effects were probably used onstage, too.

Key fact

There are no surviving plans of the Globe Theatre, but a picture and description of the Swan Theatre, similar to the Globe, did survive (see page 7).

Backstage

Backstage there was a "tiring house", where actors changed into their costumes and were given their props (see page 18).

They came onstage through doors (there was no stage curtain). Outside, doormen collected the entrance money in boxes, which is where we get the term "box office".

Did you know?

The groundlings who stood in the pit were sometimes nicknamed "stinkards", because the actors could smell them from the stage.

By Royal Command

At Christmas or on special occasions theatre companies performed for the monarch or for grand noblemen. We know that William Shakespeare sometimes wrote plays for these royal events.

Nobles gather for a performance by a visiting theatre company.

Important audience

The play would take place in a royal palace or a grand house. The audience of nobles sat in a room lit by candles, and the actors came in and out of the room's doors. It was important to keep the monarch and nobles happy, otherwise a company could be banned from working or even thrown in jail.

Did you know?

Acting companies were paid a fee of £10 for a royal performance, much more than they earned on a normal day.

Tudor-style fame

Successful actors and playwrights were celebrities in Elizabethan times and nobles did not mind mixing with them. After a Court performance, the main theatre actors would probably be invited to dine with the nobles themselves. The lesser actors would be invited to eat in the kitchens.

A picture of how Elizabeth I and her courtiers might have watched a play being performed in a grand house.

The theatre company

The Chamberlain's Men are the most famous Elizabethan company of actors, because their playwright was William Shakespeare.

Richard Burbage managed the Chamberlain's Men.

In the company

The co-owners of an acting company were called "sharers". William Shakespeare was a sharer in the Chamberlain's Men, along with the main actors and the manager.

Key fact

The star actors shared in the profits of the theatre and probably had a say in the way plays were performed.

 Did you know?

A jig (a funny dance) was performed as an extra show at the end of a comic play.

The manager

The company manager paid for plays to be written, chose the right actors for the parts and organised performances. The manager of Shakespeare's company was Richard Burbage, who also acted and even painted the sets.

Stars of the show

The star actors had parts written especially for them. In Shakespeare's company the most famous actor was Will Kempe, who was a comic star famous for performing funny dances called jigs.

Go and visit

A theatre workshop for children, where you can try your hand at being an actor. Most theatres run these, so look out for one near you.

 Did you know?

Occasionally actors were accidentally stabbed to death during sword-fights on stage.

Boys on stage

It was against the law for women or girls to perform onstage in Tudor times.

Acting apprentices

Boys took on the female roles, training to talk and act like women. Noblemen of the time had long hair and dressed in fine embroidered clothes and jewellery, so it wasn't seen as all that unusual for a male to dress in female clothes.

Childrens' companies

A few acting and singing companies were made up of children. For instance, The Children of St Paul's performed in a house near St Paul's Cathedral.

Queen Elizabeth also had her own group of choristers (boy singers) who sang and performed for her.

All boys wore dresses until the age of five in Tudor times.

Growing up

When a boy actor grew up and his voice got deep, his career as a child actor was over. If he was good enough, he might become an adult actor, but there was no guarantee because his adult voice might turn out to be too weak for the stage.

A wealthy Elizabethan woman in typical dress. Boy actors tried to make themselves look as ladylike as possible.

The theatre crowd

Watching a play at an Elizabethan theatre must have been a lively experience. The audience moved around and even joined in, if they felt like it.

Choose your seat

The balcony seats (also called "galleries") were more expensive than standing in the pit in front of the stage, so well-off people such as merchants and lawyers would probably sit there. For sixpence, men could actually sit on the side of the stage itself, perhaps to show off their fine clothes. Groundlings paid a penny to stand in the pit, which was open to the sky.

A modern performance at the Globe. If it rains, the groundlings standing in the pit get wet.

The "Lord's Room"

The "Lord's Room" was a balcony above the stage where noblemen and women sat, so they didn't have to mix with the crowd. When lords and ladies weren't at the show, the theatre musicians probably took their place in the balcony. They played music during the play.

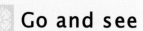

Go and see

In summer plays are performed at the modern Globe, and audiences can find out what it was like at an Elizabethan theatre.

Actors rehearse a Shakespeare play at the modern Globe Theatre.

Scandal!

Tudor theatres were scandalous places where gambling and drinking went on, and sometimes pickpockets (then called "cutpurses") stole money from the crowd. Many people thought actors were rascals who behaved badly and that theatres were wicked.

Key fact

A theatre such as the Globe could fit in over 1,000 people at a time, so it must have been very noisy and exciting.

Props and costumes

Each theatre company kept a store of costumes, scenery and props (objects needed in plays).

The tiring house

The props were kept backstage in the tiring house, which was also the actors' dressing room. The "tire-man" (wardrobe master) looked after them and on the day of a play he made sure that everything was ready for the actors. Elizabethan stages didn't have big background scenery. Instead there were small moveable pieces, such as model trees or bushes.

Costumes help an audience to understand the part an actor is playing.

Costumes

The actors wore normal Elizabethan clothes, never imaginative made-up costumes or outfits from a different time in history, as actors do nowadays. Sometimes a theatre company bought second-hand clothes from nobles, to use on stage.

Did you know?

Tudor theatres used real cannons to provide special effects. In 1613, a cannon set fire to the thatched roof of the Globe and it burnt to the ground.

When Tudor plays are performed at the modern Globe Theatre, the costumes are often in the style of Shakespeare's time.

Props of the Admiral's Men

A list of props has survived from the Admiral's Men, a theatre company of the time. The list includes all kinds of surprising objects, such as a cage, a tree of golden apples, Neptune's fork, a rainbow, a bull's head and a dragon! There were several crowns and weapons, and even a "black dog".

Key fact

Playwrights built props into the plays they wrote. Shakespeare's play *Hamlet* uses a famous prop — a skull held up by the actors.

Go and visit

The backstage area of a theatre, to see props and dressing rooms. Most theatres run tours, including the home of the Royal Shakespeare Company in Shakespeare's home town, Stratford-upon-Avon.

The plays

The theatre companies paid playwrights to write new plays for them.

Taking a copy

Playwrights wrote with a quill, a bird's feather dipped in a pot of ink. Very few copies were made of new plays, and they were very valuable to a theatre company. Sometimes they were illegally copied and sold, rather like pirate CDs and films today.

Actors and their lines

The actors were given their own part written out separately and stuck on a long piece of parchment. They never had the whole play to read, only their own lines. If they forgot their lines onstage, somebody would prompt them (remind them what to say), just as stage prompters do today.

Joseph Fiennes uses a quill pen in a scene from the film Shakespeare in Love.

Key fact

English in Shakespeare's time was not the same as modern English, and the plays are sometimes hard for today's readers to understand. Modern copies have lots of footnotes that explain what words mean.

Plays worth millions

During Shakespeare's lifetime his plays were printed in pamphlets called quartos. They are the nearest thing we now have to the original writings, which are now lost. The *First Folio*, the first known printed collection of Shakespeare's plays, was published in 1623 after he died. Early Shakespeare quartos and folios are now worth millions of pounds because they are so rare.

The title page of the First Folio *edition of Shakespeare's plays from the British Library.*

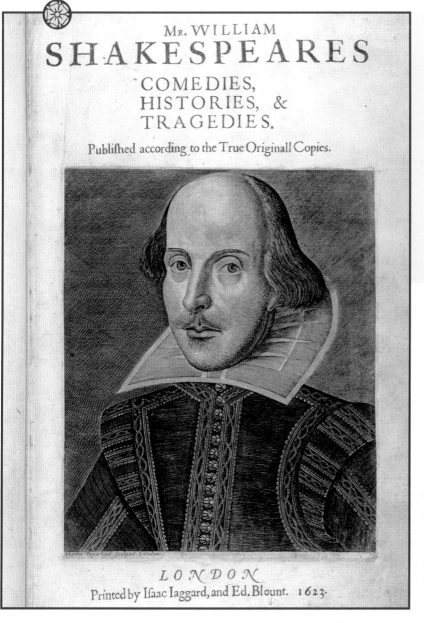

MR. WILLIAM

SHAKESPEARES

COMEDIES,
HISTORIES, &
TRAGEDIES.

Publifhed according to the True Originall Copies.

LONDON
Printed by Ifaac Iaggard, and Ed. Blount. 1623.

Go and visit

The British Library website at www.bl.uk, where you can see photos of priceless Shakespeare folios and quartos.

Did you know?

Some of the most famous of Shakespeare's lines vary between quarto copies. Nobody is sure which are inaccurate versions made up later.

William Shakespeare

William Shakespeare wrote history plays, comedies and tragedies, and also wrote short poems called sonnets.

Is this the face of William Shakespeare? This could be a portrait of the playwright, but nobody is certain.

Young Shakespeare

Shakespeare was born in Stratford-upon-Avon in Warwickshire in 1564. His father was a glove-maker and his mother was a farmer's daughter. Shakespeare probably went to grammar school, where he would have learned to read and write Latin. He married and had children before he went to London to be an actor and a playwright, leaving his family behind.

Key fact

Shakespeare was a celebrity in his day. His plays were particularly liked by Elizabeth I and James I. After his death, his reputation kept growing.

Acting and writing

In 1594 Shakespeare joined the Chamberlain's Men and got a patron (important supporter), a powerful nobleman called the Earl of Southampton. For the next twenty years he was with the Chamberlain's Men — as their regular playwright. In 1614, he went back to Stratford-upon-Avon and died there two years later.

What did he look like?

We don't know for sure what Shakespeare looked like. Several famous pictures of him were done many years after his death, so could well be wrong. Most pictures show him with a high forehead, curly dark hair and a moustache.

 Did you know?

Some scholars insist that William Shakespeare could not have written the plays which carry his name. They think he was too badly educated, and a nobleman must have written them.

A statue of Shakespeare in Westminster Abbey, London.

 Go and visit

The tomb of William Shakespeare in Stratford-upon-Avon. In the same town you can visit some of the houses connected with his family.

Shakespeare's rivals

Shakespeare was not the only Elizabethan playwright. There were several others, including Christopher Marlowe and Ben Jonson.

Marlowe, murdered star

Marlowe was a famous actor and playwright, and his plays are still performed today. In 1593 he was stabbed to death at a house in Deptford, near London. Some people think he was murdered because he may have been a government spy.

Christopher Marlowe. Some people think his death was faked and that he lived in Italy for many years.

Key fact

Ben Jonson trained as a bricklayer before he became an actor. Christopher Marlowe was the son of a Canterbury shoemaker. Just like Shakespeare, they gained success through their talent, but they all had the help of noble patrons, as well.

Ben Jonson

Ben Jonson was known for his satires — lively rude plays that poked fun at people. He was an actor, too, and once accidentally killed another actor in a stage fight. In his writings he mentions that Shakespeare was proud of the fact that he never made a blot on his writing. Jonson rudely joked that he wished Shakespeare had blotted out more of his work! But he was probably Shakespeare's friend.

An engraving of a portrait of Ben Jonson.

 Go and visit

The National Portrait Gallery in London. Visit the website, www.npg.org.uk, to see 30 portraits of Shakespeare.

Playwright teams

Shakespeare sometimes wrote plays with other playwrights. This was probably not unusual for the times, when playwrights often wrote together to get plays done quickly. His final three plays were written with a young writer called John Fletcher.

 Marlowe and Jonson

Marlowe's plays are very bloodthirsty, and full of secret plotting and murders. Ben Jonson's plays are violent, too, but they have lots of very rude jokes in them.

Danger!

It was very dangerous to upset a monarch in Shakespeare's time. Theatre companies had to be very careful not to perform plays that might offend.

Essex brings trouble

Shakespeare's main patron, the Earl of Southampton, was a friend of the powerful Earl of Essex. In 1600 the Earl of Essex was banned from the Court of Elizabeth I, and began plotting against the Queen's advisors. It was a dangerous time for all his friends, including Shakespeare and the Chamberlain's Men.

A risky performance

The Chamberlain's Men performed a play, Shakespeare's *Richard the Second*, for Essex and his supporters. Soon after the

The Earl of Essex had been a close friend of Elizabeth I. However, he plotted to get more power, and was eventually executed.

performance, Essex and his men marched through the streets of London, demanding rebellion against the Queen's advisors. The march failed and Essex was imprisoned and executed. Shakespeare and his theatre company could have been banned for their link to Essex, but they were lucky.

The Earl of Southampton, Shakespeare's patron, was a friend of the Earl of Essex.

Did you know?

The Chamberlain's Men were commanded to perform at Court on the evening before the execution of the Earl of Essex.

Go and visit

The Tower of London, where Essex was imprisoned and executed on 25 February 1601. Shakespeare was lucky to avoid a spell in jail there.

Banned!

Elizabeth I died in 1603, and the London theatres closed for a while as a sign of respect.

A rowdy crowd

Elizabeth's successor, James I, liked the theatre and at the beginning of his reign, Shakespeare was more popular than ever. Gradually, however, the nobles at Court grew more wild and out-of-control. Performances at Court must have been lively and noisy, with drunken courtiers shouting out at the actors as they played their parts.

Masques became popular in the early 1600s. This picture shows a masque taking place in the great hall of a large house.

The end of the acting

During James's reign, and under his successor Charles I, masques became more popular than plays at Court. A masque was an evening of music, poems and dancing, in which women of the Court could take part.

The Puritans

The theatres were closed during the Civil Wars of the 1640s. Then they were destroyed by the Puritans. The rebuilt Globe was closed in 1642 and pulled down two years later. The modern Globe, below, stands on the south bank of the River Thames in London.

Key fact

English Puritans of the time thought that acting was sinful. They banned it when they won the Civil Wars, and no-one acted again until Charles II came to the throne in 1660. He allowed women to appear on stage for the first time.

Go and visit

The Theatre Museum in Covent Garden, London, or see their collection of theatre history at www.peopleplayuk.org.uk.

Glossary

backstage
The area hidden behind a theatre stage, where props and costumes are kept ready, and where actors wait.

City of London
An area of London on the northern bank of the River Thames.

Chamberlain's Men
Shakespeare's theatre company, who performed at the Globe.

company
A group of actors who regularly work together in a theatre.

Court
The family and nobles close to the king or queen.

Elizabethan
During the reign of Elizabeth I, from 1558 to 1603.

folio
A printed collection of Shakespeare's plays.

galleries
Balconies around the inside of a theatre, for the audience.

Globe, the
The theatre that William Shakespeare co-owned.

groundlings
Members of the audience who stood in front of the stage.

masque
An evening of poetry, music and dancing.

patron
A wealthy important person who supported a theatre company.

quarto
A printed pamphlet version of a Shakespeare play.

plague
A deadly disease spread by fleas.

props
Objects used during a play.

Puritans
Religious extremists of the 1600s.

quarto
A printed pamphlet version of a Shakespeare play.

Southwark
An area of London on the south bank of the River Thames.

sharers
Co-owners of a theatre.

tiring house
A backstage area where props and costumes were kept and where actors dressed in their costumes.

touring
When an acting company travels around, putting on plays.

tragedy
A play where the main character has a flaw that results in disaster.

Tudor
The name of the family who ruled England for 118 years, including Henry VII, Henry VIII, Edward VI, Mary I and Elizabeth I.

Timeline

1485 Henry Tudor defeats Richard III at the Battle of Bosworth Field. He is crowned King.

1558 Elizabeth I is crowned Queen, the fifth Tudor monarch.

1564 William Shakespeare is born in Stratford-upon-Avon.

1576 The first theatre is built in England.

1582 Shakespeare marries Anne Hathaway.

1583 Shakespeare's daughter, Susanna, is born.

1585 Shakespeare's twins, Hamnet and Judith, are born.

1593 Christopher Marlowe is killed in Deptford.

1595 Shakespeare performs in front of the Queen.

1596 Shakespeare's son, Hamnet, dies aged 11.

1599 The Globe Theatre opens.

1601 The Earl of Essex is executed.

1603 Queen Elizabeth I dies and James I becomes king. He is from the Stuart family, so the Tudor era comes to an end.

1608 The Chamberlain's Men, now renamed the King's Men, open an indoor theatre at Blackfriars.

1613 The Globe burns down, but it is rebuilt.

1616 Shakespeare dies.

1642 The rebuilt Globe is closed.

1660 Charles II comes to the throne.

1997 The reconstruction of the Globe is completed on Bankside.

Websites

www.shakespearesglobe.com/
The website of the reconstructed Globe Theatre.

www.rsc.org.uk
The website of the Royal Shakespeare Company, who perform in London and Stratford-upon-Avon. Find out about their work.

www.shakespeare.org.uk
Find out all about Shakespeare's life and his birthplace.

www.kes.net/about-us/ history-of-the-school/
The website of the school where Shakespeare was a pupil.

www.nationaltrust.org.uk
Find out about Tudor places to visit near you.

www.britinfo.net/theatre/
Find a weblink to your local theatre, to see what's on and how you can join in.

Index